~MY~ QUEST FOR EXCELLENCE

WORKBOOK

DR. CLIFFORD E. DAUGHERTY

QUEST INSTITUTE FOR QUALITY EDUCATION

~MY~
QUEST
FOR EXCELLENCE

WORKBOOK

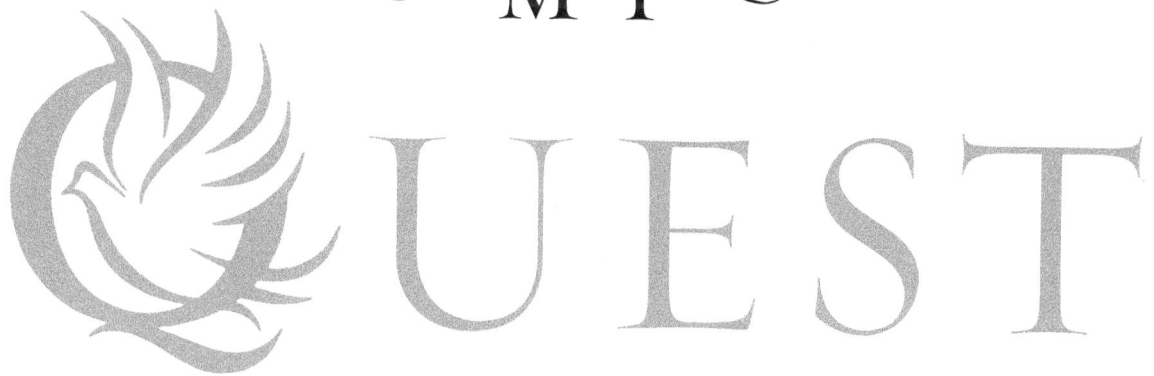

QUEST *for* EXCELLENCE | MEDIA

My Quest for Excellence Workbook

Copyright © 2015 by Clifford E. Daugherty, Ed.D.

Published by Quest for Excellence Media
100 Skyway Drive
San Jose CA 95111
408-513-2503

The phrases "Quest for Excellence," "Excellence Brings Influence," and "Quest Institute" throughout this book are trademarked by Valley Christian Schools.

Library of Congress Cataloging-in-Publication Data

Daugherty, Clifford E.
    My quest for excellence workbook / Clifford E. Daugherty, Ed. D.
p. cm.

ISBN: 978-0-9964207-7-8

Printed in the United States of America

Photo by Nathan Ngo (Valley Christian High School photography student)
Design by Peter Gloege | LOOK Design Studio

TABLE OF CONTENTS

— ALSO BY —

DR. CLIFFORD E. DAUGHERTY

QUEST FOR EXCELLENCE
Paperback: ISBN: 978-0-9964207-0-9
eBook: ISBN: 978-0-9964207-1-6
Audio: ISBN: 978-0-9964207-5-4

THE QUEST CONTINUES
Paperback: ISBN: 978-0-9964207-2-3
eBook: ISBN: 978-0-9964207-3-0
Audio: ISBN: 978-0-9964207-4-7

WWW.QUESTFOREXCELLENCEMEDIA.COM

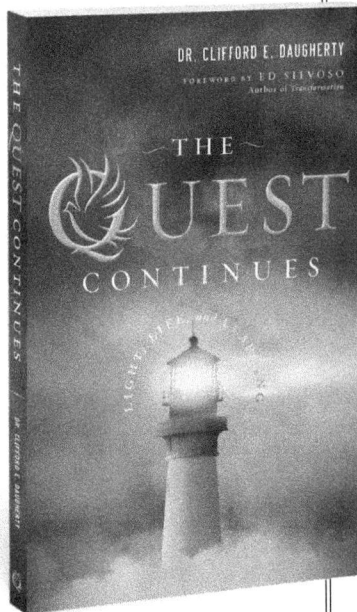

INTRODUCTION

My *Quest for Excellence Workbook* is a tool to assist *Quest for Excellence* readers in pursuing their personal Quests for Excellence. The material in this workbook explores the Twenty Indispensable Principles as found in Chapter 22 of *Quest for Excellence* as well as the "Reflections" at the back of its sequel, *The Quest Continues*. This guide is designed for use as a road map for personal growth by individuals, groups, or book clubs.

After a recap of the twenty principles, the first lesson of this workbook makes a careful study of the nature of excellence, material taken from Chapters 8 and 9 of *The Quest Continues*. The twenty principles are then grouped over the next five lessons for closer examination. Each of the six lessons includes questions relating to the principles of excellence, with space for personal written reflections and action plans.

The end of the workbook provides space to record "My Personal Quest for Excellence Written Vision Statement," with summaries of the vision God is revealing for the next one, three, and ten or more years.

"UNLESS THE LORD

BUILDS THE HOUSE,

THEY LABOR IN VAIN

WHO BUILD IT . . ."

PSALM 127:1

HOW TO HAVE FAITH FOR THE IMPOSSIBLE AND EXPERIENCE GOD'S SUPERNATURAL WORK— NATURALLY

Throughout our faith journey, we at Valley Christian Schools have learned many faith lessons about living a supernatural life naturally. God has accomplished His wonderful works through us even when it seemed impossible. These principles have timeless truth for anyone desiring to have faith to pursue God unwaveringly, pray persistently, and witness His amazing involvement in everyday life.

We believe the power of God is available to anyone who will seek Him on His terms. We can never put a leash on God to lead Him where we want to go. On the contrary, the key to experiencing His power is to surrender ourselves to the Lord for His purposes, dying to ourselves and inviting the excellence of Christ to live through us—supernaturally.

Here are some of the lessons I've learned through God's amazing miraculous works at Valley Christian Schools.

1. GET TO KNOW "THE BOSS"

Devote yourself to knowing God at increasingly deeper levels. The more you get to know His nature, character, and works, the more He will accomplish His supernatural work through you—naturally.

2. STAY IN THE BOOK

Feed your soul on God's written Word. Maintain high regard for God's ability to guide and direct through the eternal principles of scripture. Memorize passages so God can use them to speak to you at any time. I have committed to reading God's Word for at least five minutes every day. Five minutes often leads to much more time. When I read, I am praying for God to direct me personally through His Holy Spirit. The Word of God is alive, and He will personalize parts of scripture that seem to joyfully scream at you as though God is speaking to you alone. God will use His words in the Bible to guide you through an adventurous journey as you follow Jesus and the leading of His Holy Spirit.

3. STAY TUNED AND KEEP TALKING

Pray regularly as a spiritual discipline. Give God your full attention so He has an opportunity to speak to you about anything, including matters not already on your mind. As you develop a God-consciousness in all you do, you will find it easier to keep your ear tuned to God's Spirit and maintain a dialog with Him throughout the day. Listen for God to speak into your thoughts in every situation. Even if the answer seems obvious, He most likely has something to say, if only to confirm your thoughts. He may surprise you. These adventures with the Lord will become amazing testimonies of God's miraculous works. Be sure to disclose those supernatural works to inspire others to follow Jesus.

4. GET A HEART TRANSPLANT

Allow God to transplant His thoughts, desires, and purposes into your heart. Be willing to let go of previous assumptions and practices, even those long held. In particular, do not confuse personal or cultural preferences with timeless Christian principles.

> *"And I will give you a new heart with new and right desires, and I will put a new spirit in you. I will take out your stony heart of sin and give you a new, obedient heart. And I will put my Spirit in you so you will obey my laws and do whatever I command"* (Ezekiel 36:26–27, NLT).

5. WALK IN THE LIGHT

Ask God to shine the light of His Holy Spirit on any area of your heart in need of house-cleaning. Ask Jesus to clean house by immediately confessing trespasses. Submit to God's will, and stay in right relationship with Him moment by moment so nothing blocks your communication. Keep in proper submission to people who have spiritual authority over you. Make sure all your personal, family, and business relationships are in order, since the kingdom of God is a kingdom of righteous, loving relationships with God, our neighbors, and ourselves.

6. GET A CLUE!

Understand that a God-given vision is getting a glimpse of what God wants to do through you. When God gives you a vision, He will give the faith and the means to see it happen as you follow Him.

7. THINK BIG

Expect that any vision from God is going to be bigger than any dream you could ever imagine. Depend on God's resources rather than what you have on hand or in view. If you can see your way clear to accomplish the vision, it is probably not of God.

8. MISSION IMPOSSIBLE?

Don't dismiss "impossible" options. Likewise, do not assume that the opening of promising new doors means God wants you to walk through them. Pray and ask God to confirm His direction.

9. EXPECT CONFIRMATION

God sometimes confirms His message through a persistent, deeper sense of "knowing," or He may speak through scripture reading or various circumstances of life. On occasion, He confirms His guidance through other people, and often through a combination of means. When you sense God is speaking, do not be afraid to ask Him for confirmation and correct understanding. Once you receive confirmation and correct understanding, move ahead in courage to obey what you have heard. When you have confidence about God's will for a particular situation, it becomes easier to persist in prayer, faith, and action toward its accomplishment. An often-repeated pattern for me is:

A. Confirmation through a passage of scripture that seems to come alive

B. Support from my wife, Kris, or other loved ones

C. The presence of a prayer burden for the project by our intercessory prayer group

D. Agreement by our administrative team and our Valley Christian Schools board

10. LET GOD SPEAK FOR HIMSELF

Do not be surprised when you cannot convince others to support a God-sized project. After all, a rational person might tell you God's plans seem impossible. Trust that He knows how to communicate with people who are needed for the project in ways personally meaningful to them.

11. PAY THE PRICE

As God leads, be willing to sacrifice and give all toward the fulfillment of His purposes. When God wants to stretch your faith, the process is often uncomfortable, or even painful, requiring you to see and do things differently and seemingly unnaturally. It is not unusual for you, a rational person, to question your sanity; after all, Noah built an ark on dry ground when it had never rained in the history of the world. Or perhaps you resonate with Moses, who was tasked with leading millions of people across the Red Sea without a single boat; or with aged Abraham and barren Sarah trying to have as many children as there are stars in the sky and grains of sand on the seashore. Trust Him to take care of your needs and your reputation in pursuit of the vision. Take heed: The more vision God gives, the more you are responsible to accomplish what He has shown you. As Jesus said, ". . . to whom much is given, from him much will be required" (Luke 12:48).

12. WAIT UPON THE LORD

Since only God can do His work, "wait on the Lord" to do it. You cannot force progress even if you try. Position yourself for God to act, then watch and wait expectantly for what God will do. Allow time for God to do His work in His way. Allow Him to teach you through trials and challenges. Wait, but do not give up on the vision. God often gives progressive disclosure to His vision. Oftentimes, the larger the vision, the longer the lead time between seeing the vision and doing the vision. The lead time allows for adequate prayer, personal spiritual growth, and planning.

We were led to purchase the land for Valley Christian Schools ten years before God opened the door for city approvals and for construction to begin. The Skyway campus vision seemed dead and buried. But about the time I began to question whether I had misunderstood God's vision, God powerfully resurrected the project. I have discovered that God often allows all to appear lost right before He shows up and does His miraculous work. I call them "Cliff hangers"! It is a great reminder that He is God and He uses these circumstances to grow our faith.

13. FORGET PLAN B

Insist on going forward according to God's "A Team" plans. When obstacles or set-backs arise, pray and ask God to show you how He wants to deal with the situation. Believe that He does not want to settle for Plan B. Do not succumb to fear. God's vision is never lacking His provision. Be open to creative and unprecedented solutions. Remember, "Plans made in heaven are never ten feet too short!" (a Chapter 11 reference).

14. CALL IN THE AIR FORCE

The Bible refers to Satan as "the mighty prince of the power of the air" (Ephesians 2:2, NLT). The enemy always opposes God's work. Remember Paul's admonition: "For we are not fighting against people made of flesh and blood, but against the evil rulers and authorities of the unseen world, against those mighty powers of darkness who rule this world, and against wicked spirits in the heavenly realms" (Ephesians 6:12, NLT).

God appoints prayer intercessors to call in the "air cover" of His angelic hosts for His faithful warriors on the front lines. Watch for and honor the intercessors God assigns to pray for you and the vision you share. It is very helpful to pray weekly with an intercessory team as God leads. Keep your prayer team informed of your vision, your prayer requests, and how God is answering prayer, so they can pray strategically. Allow God to guide corporately as well as individually. "Pray at all times and on every occasion in the power of the Holy Spirit. Stay alert and be persistent in your prayers for all Christians everywhere. And pray for me, too" (Ephesians 6:18–19a, NLT).

The enemy is no match for God's angelic air force, and the Lord will defeat "the mighty prince of the power of the air" through prayer and the air cover of His angelic hosts. Every phase of God's work at Valley Christian Schools required a breakthrough in prayer to achieve success. When circumstances, human weaknesses, and dark forces seem to block God's purposes, partner with God-appointed prayer intercessors to call in the air force—God's angelic hosts!

"Praise Him, all His angels; praise Him, all His hosts!"
(Psalm 148:2).

"Restore us, O Lord God of hosts; cause Your face to shine,
and we shall be saved!" (Psalm 80:19).

"The Lord of hosts is with us; the God of Jacob
is our refuge" (Psalm 46:11).

God assigns His angels to watch over us as children, and they are at His command to help us achieve His purposes throughout our lives as we pray and seek to serve Him. "See that you don't look down on one of these little ones, because I tell you that in heaven their angels continually view the face of My Father in heaven" (Matthew 18:10, HCSB).

(If you would like to study the subject of angels in more depth, see Billy Graham's book *Angels, Angels, Angels*.)

15. KEEP THE FAITH

Do not allow obstacles to stop you or to damage your faith. Your faith will soar if instead you see obstacles as opportunities for God to demonstrate His miraculous power. Let Him reassure you about His desire and intention to accomplish His highest purposes in whatever way He chooses. Faith is a gift of the Holy Spirit, and God gives us the gift for each of His works. We cannot manufacture miracle-working faith. "The Spirit gives special faith . . ." (1 Corinthians 12:9, NLT).

16. DUKE IT OUT

Give yourself permission to wrestle with your doubts and to work through the "why" questions. Ask God to help you understand scriptural truths that apply to your situation. Ask God for the faith to make a wholehearted commitment to move forward in the face of unanswered questions like, "Where will we get the money?"

17. TAP GREAT TALENT

Ask God to help you do the homework needed to discover and engage the finest talent to help move the vision forward. Ask "the Lord of the harvest to send out laborers into His harvest" (Luke 10:2). The initial price tag is usually higher, but quality usually improves the bottom line before long.

18. NO SECRETS

Always share the vision God gave you with those who will listen. On more than one occasion, I have shared God's vision with people of seemingly modest means who eventually gave tens of thousands—and even millions—of dollars in response to God's leading. Be faithful to share the vision, but understand that it is only God who can lead people to give their time, talent, and treasure from their hearts.

19. AIM FOR THE STARS

Aim for excellence in everything you do. Ultimately, true excellence is the nature, character, and works of God. Anything we do truly reflecting excellence requires the work of God and is by definition "supernatural." Pursuing His excellence opens the door to experiencing His supernatural works in your everyday life—naturally.

20. JOURNAL THE JOURNEY

Periodically document the ways God has supernaturally worked through your life. Honor Him for His faithfulness, and allow these accounts to bring you and others into a new dimension of faith in and love for God. Later in life when you face doubts and difficulties, written testimonies of what God has accomplished through you will be a great encouragement. Recorded details of God's miraculous works will speak to you, your children, and their children, and teach others about His faithfulness.

LESSON ONE

". . . Excellent Glory . . ."
— 2 PETER 1:17

T he power of the Quest for Excellence caused me to reflect more deeply on its meaning. Why and how are the Quest for Excellence and the Excellence Brings Influence strategy so powerful at Valley Christian Schools? As I prayed for answers, scriptures came alive to me in new ways, and I set out to discover all the verses in the Bible speaking of *excellence* in relation to God's nature, character, or works (as described in *Quest for Excellence* on pages 33, 58–59, 60–61, 64, 181, 192, 229, 233, 238, and 247 of the 2015 edition). I found eleven verses in the New King James Version with nine different descriptions of God's excellence. At first I simply listed the eleven verses in nine rows describing nine references to excellence about God. In the following table, the nine descriptions of God's excellence are in the left column, their Bible verses are in the middle column, and the Bible verse references appear in the right column:

BIBLE VERSES PRESENTING NINE DESCRIPTIONS OF GOD'S EXCELLENCE (NKJV)

Excellent Greatness	The **greatness** of Your **excellence** . . . Praise Him for His mighty acts; praise Him according to His **excellent greatness**!	Exodus 15:7 Psalm 150:2
Excellent Name	O LORD, our Lord, how **excellent is Your name** in all the earth! Having become so much better than the angels, as He has by inheritance obtained a more **excellent name** than they.	Psalm 8:1, 9 Hebrews 1:4
Excellent Guidance	This also comes from the LORD of hosts, who is wonderful in counsel and **excellent in guidance**.	Isaiah 28:29
Excellent Way	But earnestly desire the best gifts. And yet I show you a more **excellent way**. [The way of love – God is love]	1 Corinthians 12:31
Excellent Power	But we have this treasure in earthen vessels, that the **excellence of the power** may be of God and not of us.	2 Corinthians 4:7
Excellent Things	Sing to the LORD, for He has done **excellent things**; this is known in all the earth.	Isaiah 12:5
Excellent Knowledge	Yet indeed I also count all things loss for the **excellence of the knowledge** of Christ Jesus my Lord, for whom I have suffered the loss of all things, and count them as rubbish, that I may gain Christ.	Philippians 3:8
Excellent Ministry	But now He has obtained a more **excellent ministry**, inasmuch as He is also Mediator of a better covenant, which was established on better promises.	Hebrews 8:6
Excellent Glory	For He received from God the Father honor and glory when such a voice came to Him from the **Excellent Glory**: "This is My beloved Son, in whom I am well pleased."	2 Peter 1:17

Table from *The Quest Continues*, p. 126

> "FOR HE RECEIVED FROM
> GOD THE FATHER HONOR AND GLORY
> WHEN SUCH A VOICE CAME TO
> HIM FROM THE EXCELLENT GLORY:
> 'THIS IS MY BELOVED SON,
> IN WHOM I AM WELL PLEASED.'"
>
> —2 PETER 1:17

The final verse from 2 Peter 1:17 struck me in a big way. A study of the passage revealed that the capitalization of "Excellent Glory" and equivalent phrases in the NKJV, NIV, NASB, and other Bible versions is necessary because "Excellent Glory" is used by Peter as the name of our heavenly Father. Of course, it was God the Father who spoke the words quoted in the verse ("This is My beloved Son, in whom I am well pleased") at Christ's transfiguration (see Matthew 17:5). This discovery led me to complete assurance of this foundational truth: God describes Himself as the ultimate standard of excellence through His name "Excellent Glory." I became more convinced that studying the Bible's revelation of God's nature, character, and works is the key to unlocking the pipeline of His excellent works through our lives.

To better illustrate the Bible's insights on the idea of excellence as revealed in the nature, character, and works of God, I further developed the table by adding a fourth column on the far left side identifying these three excellence categories. The verses describing God's excellence are then redistributed to match the categories of God's nature, character, and works. The column listing the excellent attributes of God as named in the verses also adds descriptors corresponding to each attribute of excellence:

BIBLE VERSES PRESENTING SEVEN CATEGORIES OF EXCELLENCE IN RELATION TO THE NATURE, CHARACTER, AND WORKS OF GOD (NKJV)

GOD'S NATURE	**Omnipotence** Greatness Power Glory **Omnipresence**	The **greatness** of Your **excellence** . . .	Exodus 15:7
		Praise Him for His mighty acts; praise Him according to His excellent **greatness**!	Psalm 150:2
		But we have this treasure in earthen vessels, that the **excellence of the power** may be of God and not of us.	2 Corinthians 4:7
		For He received from God the Father honor and glory when such a voice came to Him from the **Excellent Glory:** "This is My beloved Son, in whom I am well pleased."	2 Peter 1:17
	Omniscience Knowledge	Yet indeed I also count all things loss for the **excellence of the knowledge** of Christ Jesus my Lord, for whom I have suffered the loss of all things, and count them as rubbish, that I may gain Christ.	Philippians 3:8
GOD'S CHARACTER	**Holiness** Name	O LORD, our Lord, how **excellent is Your name** in all the earth!	Psalm 8:1, 9
		Having become so much better than the angels, as He has by inheritance obtained a more **excellent name** than they.	Hebrews 1:4
GOD'S WORKS	**Creator** Things	Sing to the LORD, for He has done **excellent things**; this is known in all the earth.	Isaiah 12:5
	Counselor Guidance	This also comes from the LORD of hosts, who is wonderful in counsel and **excellent in guidance.**	Isaiah 28:29
	Savior Way	But earnestly desire the best gifts. And yet I show you a more **excellent way.** [The way of love – Jesus is the Way]	1 Corinthians 12:31
	Mediator Ministry	But now He has obtained a more **excellent ministry,** inasmuch as He is also Mediator of a better covenant, which was established on better promises.	Hebrews 8:6

Table from *The Quest Continues*, p. 128

DR. CLIFFORD E. DAUGHERTY

As I studied the Bible verses describing the three categories of excellence in relation to the nature, character, and works of God, I reflected on my own experience in learning the difference between *knowing of* God and getting to *really know* God. Memories of early struggles to work "for God" rather than allowing God to work through me also came to mind.

Yes, I thought. *This table is very insightful.* To even begin to approach excellence by God's standards, the journey must begin with learning about God's excellent nature. Then to really understand His excellence, we must learn how to know God personally. Then, by God's grace, we become a candidate for the Divine Creator to perform His excellent works through our lives.

Jesus affirmed: "Most assuredly, I say to you, he who believes in Me, the works that I do he will do also; and greater works than these he will do, because I go to My Father. And whatever you ask in My name, that I will do, that the Father may be glorified in the Son. If you ask anything in My name, I will do it" (John 14:12–14).

My study of Christ's teachings regarding asking for "anything in My name" brought me to the insight that "in My name" means according to the will and purposes of Jesus Christ as Lord, including His ultimate purposes for His creation of the universe and all of us.

Jesus, our Creator, further developed this idea that *His* works can become *our* works in His teaching about the vine and the branches. He said, "Abide in Me, and I in you. As the branch cannot bear fruit of itself, unless it abides in the vine, neither can you, unless you abide in Me. I am the vine, you are the branches. He who abides in Me, and I in him, bears much fruit; for without Me you can do nothing" (John 15:4–5).

Abiding in Christ Jesus is the best strategic position I can imagine to get to know Him and His Excellent Glory intimately! That would be like moving into the White House and Oval Office to learn about the nature and powers of the president. In such close quarters, I could observe the president's true character and have an insightful personal opinion about whether his word can be trusted. He, too, could observe me closely. If I were appointed as the Secretary of State, I could even speak and act with the power of the president when authorized.

Oh, but Jesus, the ultimate "Excellent Glory," is so much closer than a housemate or a trusted colleague! He proposes much more than a mere mortal appointment as Secretary of State. His invitation is to "Abide in Me, and I in you," and as He enters our lives, He brings all of Himself. His Excellent Glory inhabits our beings, and His Excellent Greatness then surrounds us. His transformation of our hearts, souls, and minds makes it possible to follow Christ's command to "love the Lord God with all your heart, with all your soul, and with all your mind" (see Matthew 22:37) and for God to do His great creative works through us.

To better represent this journey, I added arrows to the following table, pointing from the top of the cell denoting "God's nature" through "God's character" and finally past "God's works."

"Yet indeed I also count
all things loss for the
excellence of the knowledge of
Christ Jesus my Lord,
for whom I have suffered the
loss of all things,
and count them as rubbish,
that I may gain Christ."

— Philippians 3:8

EXCELLENCE: THE NATURE, CHARACTER, AND WORKS OF GOD
THE QUEST FOR EXCELLENCE AND THE EXCELLENCE BRINGS INFLUENCE STRATEGY

	EXCELLENT	VERSES DESCRIBING EXCELLENCE	BIBLE REFERENCE
GOD'S NATURE	**Omnipotence** Greatness Power Glory **Omnipresence**	The **greatness** of Your **excellence** … Praise Him for His mighty acts; praise Him according to His excellent **greatness**! But we have this treasure in earthen vessels, that the **excellence of the power** may be of God and not of us. For He received from God the Father honor and glory when such a voice came to Him from the **Excellent Glory:** "This is My beloved Son, in whom I am well pleased."	Exodus 15:7 Psalm 150:2 2 Corinthians 4:7 2 Peter 1:17
	Omniscience Knowledge	Yet indeed I also count all things loss for the **excellence of the knowledge** of Christ Jesus my Lord, for whom I have suffered the loss of all things, and count them as rubbish, that I may gain Christ.	Philippians 3:8
GOD'S CHARACTER	**Holiness** Name God is: Holy, Good, Peaceful, Loving, Kind, Faithful, Gracious, Just, Merciful, Truthful, Unchanging, and much more	O LORD, our Lord, how **excellent is Your name** in all the earth! Having become so much better than the angels, as He has by inheritance obtained a more **excellent name** than they.	Psalm 8:1, 9 Hebrews 1:4
GOD'S WORKS (Arrows Indicate Sequence to Learn of the Lord and to Personally Get to Know Him)	**Creator** Things	Sing to the LORD, for He has done **excellent things**; this is known in all the earth.	Isaiah 12:5
	Counselor Guidance	This also comes from the LORD of hosts, who is wonderful in counsel and **excellent in guidance.**	Isaiah 28:29
	Savior Way	But earnestly desire the best gifts. And yet I show you a more **excellent way.** [The way of love – Jesus is the Way]	1 Corinthians 12:31
	Mediator Ministry	But now He has obtained a more **excellent ministry,** inasmuch as He is also Mediator of a better covenant, which was established on better promises.	Hebrews 8:6

Table from *The Quest Continues*, p. 131

TO KNOW JESUS INTIMATELY

Paul the Apostle was able to write, "I know whom I have believed and am persuaded that He is able to keep what I have committed to Him until that day" (2 Timothy 1:12). After acknowledging Jesus as Lord, Paul entrusted his entire life to Jesus. Paul's knowledge of God's nature, His personal character, and great works provided the strong foundation for Paul's personal relationship with Jesus. This intimate personal relationship allowed God to work through Paul to write about one third of the New Testament. His close relationship with Jesus made Paul confident he would never hear the dreaded words of Jesus on judgment day: "I never knew you; depart from Me, you who practice lawlessness!" (Matthew 7:23). Instead, Paul looked forward to hearing Christ say, "Well done, good and faithful servant; you were faithful over a few things, I will make you ruler over many things. Enter into the joy of your lord" (Matthew 25:21).

Ultimately, the Quest for Excellence is the quest to know Jesus and become like Him so He can do His great and excellent works through us. In the process, His desires become our desires and we seek to do His will. Then it becomes possible for the power of the Excellence Brings Influence strategy to take root in and through our personal lives. At this point, the promises for prosperity and success found in Joshua 1:7–9 and Psalm 1:1–3 become real.

As we learn of God's nature and character through His Word, prayer, and meditation, we can have a personal relationship with God leading to an amazing display of His supernatural works through our lives, including the power of His omnipotence, omnipresence, and omniscience. That's the power of the Omnis! Accessing God's wisdom and understanding ensures our true prosperity and success in accordance with His perfect will and plan for our lives. It is amazing to me how God changes our view of the true nature of prosperity and success to conform to His perspective. God's nature, character, and works are truly excellent, bringing us back full circle to the ultimate definition of excellence as the nature, character, and works of God.

GOD'S WORK IN AND THROUGH YOU

Before God works *through* you, He must do His great work *in* you. This idea is powerfully communicated by the writer of the book of Hebrews. "Now may the God of peace . . . make you complete in every good work to do His will, working in you what is well pleasing in His sight, through Jesus Christ" (Hebrews 13:20-21).

Someone once said, "the highest form of worship is work." Of course, this maxim must be qualified with "the work" being God's work, through us, by God's power. When we begin to understand the nature and character of God—including His infinite omnipotence, omnipresence, omniscience, holiness, love, and unending resources—a great truth becomes obvious. As God begins to work through a mere human being, instant transformation and transcendence is imparted to an otherwise finite mortal. As God inhabits our lives, His immortality transcends our mortality. Limitations of resources, intellect, space, time, and power no longer apply because, as Jesus said, "The things which are impossible with men are possible with God" (Luke 18:27). Truly, if God elects by His grace to create His works through us, our potential achievements are limited only by God's will, plans, and purposes. This is how ordinary people can have "Access to the Omnis" and to God's divine resources.

Even Jesus limited His great works to His Father's will. Such was the case when Jesus prayed to His Father in agony, "Not My will, but Yours, be done" while facing the cross (Luke 22:42). This truth was also evident when Jesus taught His disciples to pray, "Your will be done on earth as it is in heaven" (Luke 11:2). Jesus declared that He did only what was in harmony with His heavenly Father's purposes (see John 5:19).

Learning to know God personally by meditating upon His Word leads to a great opportunity to love God by keeping His commandments. Jesus said, "You shall love the Lord your God with all your heart, with all your soul, and with all your mind" (Matthew 22:37). He also said, "If you love Me, keep My commandments" and "He who has My commandments and keeps them, it is he who loves Me. And he who loves Me will be loved by My Father, and I will love him and manifest Myself to him" (John 14:15, 21).

How profound! We love Jesus by keeping His commands! The Father loves those who keep Jesus' commands. And Jesus promises to love and manifest Himself to those who keep His commands. There we have it: a personal disclosure of the Creator of the Universe to mere mortals of His own creation! Can you imagine what those ingenious creative manifestations involve? For me personally, I relish every disclosure, every supernatural provision, every miraculous insight, and every provision to achieve God's purposes through my life "according to His riches in glory by Christ Jesus" (Philippians 4:19).

Dare I say it again? This is what the Quest for Excellence means. This is God's Excellence Brings Influence strategy to accomplish all of His purposes through our lives, and to fulfill the prayer Jesus taught us to pray: "Your kingdom come. Your will be done on earth as it is in heaven" (Matthew 6:10).

Yes, for me to say I can do God's works is truly absurd, but for Jesus to say "I will do it" means it is possible for Him to do anything He wants through you and me (see John 14:14). We learn more of His nature and absorb His character through "the knowledge of God" (Colossians 1:10), then we better love Him by being obedient to His commands. In this way He can "fulfill all the good pleasure of His goodness and the work of faith with power" (2 Thessalonians 1:11), works that can be attributed only to God's love, power, and grace in and through our lives.

A PICTURE OF TWO OXEN

Jesus said, "Take My yoke upon you and learn from Me, for I am gentle and lowly in heart, and you will find rest for your souls" (Matthew 11:29). Here He gives us a picture of two oxen working inside the yoke together, side by side. Thank God He is in the yoke beside me doing most of the hard pulling, so when I fail from exhaustion and weakness, omnipotent Jesus pulls with His power, and I find rest for my soul.

It is important to learn from Jesus about God's excellent greatness, power, omniscience, and love—for me and for every breathing thing He longs to redeem. What a privilege to let Jesus' all-powerful "pull" accomplish His great creative works while I cooperate and walk beside Him. This is how the Quest for Excellence is achieved supernaturally in our lives. We can attain great influence through the excellent greatness of Jesus. He is the one doing the hard pulling, alongside of us, enabling us to desire and achieve His purposes in all we do, "heartily, as to the Lord" (Colossians 3:23). This strategy gives us great advantages both in our personal lives and through the careers God chooses for us, empowering us to bring His transforming influence to our family, community, and world. In this way, then, it is true—the highest form of worship is work. That's how Excellence Brings Influence!

There is no work too hard for Jesus, and there is no price He cannot afford. He is in all His ways infinitely powerful, loving, and holy, and He is determined to achieve His excellent works through those who will but take up His yoke and walk with Him. Experiencing God's good works is a normal way of life when every step with Jesus is directed and empowered by Him.

A study of the Bible references on the following table reveals that in every instance of "good works" involving Christians in the New Testament, such works are of God—by His grace, through His power, according to His will—and are not described as the works of human beings.

"FOR IT IS GOD WHO IS
WORKING IN YOU, ENABLING YOU
BOTH TO DESIRE AND TO
WORK OUT HIS GOOD PURPOSE."

— PHILIPPIANS 2:13 (HCSB)

THE VERSE	WHO IS WORKING, OR WHOSE ABILITY?	KIND OF WORK	REFERENCE
"This is the work of God, that you believe in Him whom He sent." (Jesus speaking)	God	Believe in Him whom He sent	John 6:29
Be steadfast, immovable, always abounding in the work of the Lord, knowing that your labor is not in vain in the Lord.	Work of the Lord	Labor in the Lord	1 Corinthians 15:58
God is able to make all grace abound toward you, that you, always having all sufficiency in all things, may have an abundance for every good work.	God is able God's grace God's sufficiency God's abundance	Good work	2 Corinthians 9:8
He who has begun a good work in you will complete it until the day of Jesus Christ.	"He": referring to God; God's ability to complete	A good work in you	Philippians 1:6
Walk worthy of the Lord, fully pleasing Him, being fruitful in every good work and increasing in the knowledge of God.	In the knowledge of God	Every good work (work of God)	Colossians 1:10
That our God would count you worthy of this calling, and fulfill all the good pleasure of His goodness and the work of faith with power …	Faith of Jesus Christ; Power of God	Fulfill the good pleasure of His goodness and the work of faith	2 Thessalonians 1:11
May our Lord Jesus Christ Himself, and our God and Father … establish you in every good word and work.	Our Lord Jesus Christ Himself, and our God and Father	Establish you in every good work	2 Thessalonians 2:16–17
That the man of God may be complete, thoroughly equipped for every good work.	Be complete and thoroughly equipped by God	For every good work	2 Timothy 3:17
Make you complete in every good work to do His will, working in you what is well pleasing in His sight, through Jesus Christ.	Through Jesus Christ	Every good work to do His will	Hebrews 13:21

Table from *The Quest Continues*, p. 140

The Quest for Excellence and the Excellence Brings Influence strategy rest entirely on knowing of or about God, personally knowing God, and loving God—experiencing God's supernatural plans, works, and power to achieve all of His purposes to and through our lives.

To complete the table introduced previously, I added a column on the left to represent God's wisdom and understanding (as endorsed in Proverbs 4:5–8) and His excellent creative works through our lives.

		GOD'S EXCELLENCE	VERSES DESCRIBING EXCELLENCE	HELPFUL SCRIPTURE
INFLUENCE Prov 4:5-8 / Matt 11:29	**GOD'S NATURE**	**EXCELLENT POWER** Omnipotence God Almighty	"I know that You can do everything, and that no purpose of Yours can be withheld from You." Job 42:2 But we have this treasure in earthen vessels, that the **excellence of the power** may be of God and not of us. 2 Corinthians 4:7	Genesis 17:1 Mark 10:27 Luke 1:37 Revelation 15:3a
—LEARN OF ME— GET UNDERSTANDING & WISDOM		**EXCELLENT PRESENCE** Omnipresence Wonderful Mighty God	"Am I a God near at hand," says the Lord, "and not a God afar off? Can anyone hide himself in secret places, so I shall not see him?" says the Lord; "do I not fill heaven and earth?" says the Lord. Jeremiah 23:23–24	Psalm 139:7–10 Proverbs 15:3 Isaiah 9:6 Matthew 18:20
		EXCELLENT KNOWLEDGE Omniscience	Yet indeed I also count all things loss for the **excellence of the knowledge** of Christ Jesus my Lord, for whom I have suffered the loss of all things, and count them as rubbish, that I may gain Christ. Philippians 3:8	1 Samuel 2:3 Job 28:24 Psalm 139:4 Psalm 147:5 Colossians 2:2–3 1 John 3:19–20
		EXCELLENT GREATNESS & GLORY Most High God Everlasting Father From Everlasting Eternal Lord	The greatness of Your **excellence**. . . . Exodus 15:7 For He received from God the Father honor and glory when such a voice came to Him from the **Excellent Glory**: "This is My beloved Son, in whom I am well pleased." 2 Peter 1:17 Praise Him for His mighty acts; praise Him according to His **excellent greatness!** Psalm 150:2	Genesis 14:20 Deut. 10:14 Isaiah 9:6 Micah 5:2 Matthew 3:17 Revelation 22:13
—LOVE ME— HEART	**GOD'S CHARACTER**	**EXCELLENT NAME** God is: Holy, Good, Peaceful, Loving, Kind, Faithful, Gracious, Just, Merciful, Truthful, Unchanging, and much more	O Lord, our Lord, how **excellent is Your name** in all the earth! Psalm 8:1, 9 Having become so much better than the angels, as He has by inheritance obtained a more **excellent name** than they. Hebrews 1:4 The fruit of the Spirit is love, joy, peace, longsuffering, kindness, goodness, faithfulness, gentleness, self-control. Galatians 5:22–23	Exodus 34:6 Leviticus 20:26 1 Samuel 2:2 Psalm 99:3–5 Psalm 103:8 Malachi 3:6 Matthew 22:37 John 15:14 Luke 1:49 Romans 12:2
—YOUR WILL BE DONE— TO & THROUGH US	**GOD'S WORKS**	**EXCELLENT THINGS** Creator and Sustainer of all things and of all life Great and marvelous works	Sing to the Lord, for He has done **excellent things**; this is known in all the earth. Isaiah 12:5 That you may approve the **things that are excellent**, that you may be sincere and without offense till the day of Christ. Philippians 1:10	Genesis 1:1 Acts 17:24–28 Romans 11:33–36 Colossians 1:17 Revelation 15:3a
Arrows Indicate Sequence to Learn of the Lord and to Personally Get to Know Him		**EXCELLENT GUIDANCE** Counselor Prince of Peace	The Lord of hosts, who is wonderful in counsel and **excellent in guidance**. Isaiah 28:29	Proverbs 16:1–3, 9 Psalm 37:3–6, 23 Isaiah 9:6
		EXCELLENT WAY Redeemer and Savior	And yet I show you a more **excellent way**. [The way of love – Jesus is the Way] 1 Corinthians 12:31	Matthew 6:33 John 10:10 Revelation 15:3b
		EXCELLENT MINISTRY Mediator	But now He has obtained a more **excellent ministry**, inasmuch as He is also Mediator of a better covenant. Hebrews 8:6.	2 Corinthians 5:18 Philippians 2:13

Table from *The Quest Continues*, p. 142

Inspired by the Holy Spirit, David penned this promise: "Delight yourself also in the LORD, and He shall give you the desires of your heart" (Psalm 37:4).

Under the same Holy Spirit anointing, King Solomon concluded: "All the ways of a man are clean in his own sight, but the LORD weighs the motives. Commit your works to the LORD and your plans will be established. The LORD has made everything for its own purpose . . ." (Proverbs 16:2–4, NASB). God's insight into correct motives reveals the key unlocking all of God's excellent power. This truth is better understood by comparing this verse in both the New King James Version as well as the New American Standard Bible. The NKJV says "The LORD has made all for Himself," and the NASB "The LORD has made everything for its own purpose." Taking both versions into account uncovers the more complete intent of God's message written in the original Hebrew language.

To the extent people commit their works to the Lord, their thoughts and plans are established in harmony with their gifts and passions and the goals they were created to achieve—and all of those thoughts and plans are perfectly aligned with God's purposes. When God, the Creator and Sustainer of the heavens and the earth, transplants His thoughts and plans into our minds, all of His divine power and resources are commanded to work through us to accomplish the passionate desires He and we long to fulfill.

What an exciting way to live! The great plans and purposes of Jesus Christ, our Creator, banish all room for boredom and aimlessness in a life dedicated to Him. God's thoughts and plans are tailored for each one of us. They are as unique and special as our fingerprints, and they are measured in waves of goodness, peace, and joy. "For the Kingdom of God is . . . living a life of goodness and peace and joy in the Holy Spirit" (Romans 14:17, NLT).

PERSONAL WRITTEN REFLECTIONS

1. Based on the biblical description of excellence, how do you define excellence?

    ....

    ....

    ....

    ....

2. Can you discern differences between biblical and world-class excellence, such as the excellence of Olympic athletes? Describe. Can world-class excellence ever aspire to biblical excellence? Why or why not?

    ....

    ....

    ....

    ....

3. Describe an experience when God manifested His excellence through you. Why do you think this happened? Or, if you can't think of such an experience, describe an area of your life where God is calling you to a Quest for Excellence. What do you see as His purposes in doing so?

    ....

    ....

    ....

    ....

4. What is the difference between God's nature and God's character?

_____

_____

_____

_____

_____

5. Is it possible for followers of Christ to do God's works? Explain your answer.

_____

_____

_____

_____

_____

6. When you are nearest to the Lord in prayer, what works do you long for God to accomplish through you? Be specific. How do you think He might do this?

_____

_____

_____

_____

_____

LESSON TWO

"This is eternal life, that they may know You,
the only true God, and Jesus Christ whom You have sent."
—JOHN 17:3

N ote: The remaining five of the six lessons in this workbook will directly correlate to the twenty principles taken from Chapter 22 of *Quest for Excellence* (as well as the "Reflections" section at the back of *The Quest Continues*). The page numbers following each principle refer to the pages in *Quest for Excellence* (2015 edition) where text insets identify stories in the book illustrating that principle. As you write your personal written reflections to better define your own God-intended Quest for Excellence journey, keep in view the Five Core Educational Values described in Chapter 20, because they directly relate to every believer's personal Quest for Excellence. In abbreviated form, the Five Core Educational Values are:

1. Parents are the primary educators of their children under God.

2. All learners are uniquely gifted with God-given talent.

3. Learners learn best through positive, loving relationships.

4. Educators help students discover their unique God-given talents through comprehensive, innovative learning opportunities.

5. Educators help students develop their God-given talents to achieve their God-intended life's work.

Here are the first three of the principles you will write reflectively about:

1. GET TO KNOW "THE BOSS" – P. 33

Devote yourself to knowing God at increasingly deeper levels. The more you get to know His nature, character, and works, the more He will accomplish His supernatural work through you—naturally.

2. STAY IN THE BOOK – P. 100

Feed your soul on God's written Word. Maintain high regard for God's ability to guide and direct through the eternal principles of scripture. Memorize passages so God can use them to speak to you at any time. I have committed to reading God's Word for at least five minutes every day. Five minutes often leads to much more time. When I read, I am praying for God to direct me personally through His Holy Spirit. The Word of God is alive, and He will personalize parts of scripture that seem to joyfully scream at you as though God is speaking to you alone. God will use His words in the Bible to guide you through an adventurous journey as you follow Jesus and the leading of His Holy Spirit.

DR. CLIFFORD E. DAUGHERTY

3. STAY TUNED AND KEEP TALKING – P. 33

Pray regularly as a spiritual discipline. Give God your full attention so He has an opportunity to speak to you about anything, including matters not already on your mind. As you develop a God-consciousness in all you do, you will find it easier to keep your ear tuned to God's Spirit and maintain a dialog with Him throughout the day. Listen for God to speak into your thoughts in every situation. Even if the answer seems obvious, He most likely has something to say, if only to confirm your thoughts. He may surprise you. These adventures with the Lord will become amazing testimonies of God's miraculous works. Be sure to disclose those supernatural works to inspire others to follow Jesus.

PERSONAL WRITTEN REFLECTIONS

1. Can you recall a time when God spoke through a parent, grandparent, teacher, or other mentor to help you discern your God-given talent? Describe the occasion and what it meant to you.

    ....

    ....

    ....

    ....

2. What are your God-given talents or passions? How does God want to work through them for His glory?

    ....

    ....

    ....

    ....

3. Have you settled upon a daily plan to read and meditate on God's Word, in order to get to know "the Boss"? Describe your practices or your new plan.

    ....

    ....

    ....

    ....

4. Google the phrase "what does the word *Rhema* mean compared to the word *Logos*?" (See, for instance, http://ati.iblp.org/ati/family/articles/concepts/rhema/.) Describe a time when God gave a *rhema* word to you.

    ....

    ....

    ....

    ....

    ....

5. Describe your prayer plan to maintain a constant conversation with God. How might your prayer plan improve?

    ....

    ....

    ....

    ....

    ....

6. How do you know when God speaks to you in prayer? Read Judges 6:11–7:25. Have you had a Gideon experience? What was your fleece? If not, what do you think about testing God as Gideon did in order to be certain of His voice?

    ....

    ....

    ....

    ....

    ....

    ....

LESSON THREE

"With God's power working in us, God can do much, much more than anything we can ask or imagine."
—EPHESIANS 3:20 (NCV)

4. GET A HEART TRANSPLANT – P. 30

Allow God to transplant His thoughts, desires, and purposes into your heart. Be willing to let go of previous assumptions and practices, even those long held. In particular, do not confuse personal or cultural preferences with timeless Christian principles.

> "And I will give you a new heart with new and right desires, and I will put a new spirit in you. I will take out your stony heart of sin and give you a new, obedient heart. And I will put my Spirit in you so you will obey my laws and do whatever I command" (Ezekiel 36:26–27, NLT).

5. WALK IN THE LIGHT – P. 78

Ask God to shine the light of His Holy Spirit on any area of your heart in need of house-cleaning. Ask Jesus to clean house by immediately confessing trespasses. Submit to God's will, and stay in right relationship with Him moment by moment so nothing blocks your communication. Keep in proper submission to people who have spiritual authority over you. Make sure all your personal, family, and business relationships are in order, since the kingdom of God is a kingdom of righteous, loving relationships with God, our neighbors, and ourselves.

6. GET A CLUE! – P. 186

Understand that a God-given vision is getting a glimpse of what God wants to do through you. When God gives you a vision, He will give the faith and the means to see it happen as you follow Him.

7. THINK BIG – PP. 158, 174

Expect that any vision from God is going to be bigger than any dream you could ever imagine. Depend on God's resources rather than what you have on hand or in view. If you can see your way clear to accomplish the vision, it is probably not of God.

8. MISSION IMPOSSIBLE? – P. 140

Don't dismiss "impossible" options. Likewise, do not assume that the opening of promising new doors means God wants you to walk through them. Pray and ask God to confirm His direction.

PERSONAL WRITTEN REFLECTIONS

1. Describe a "Psalm 37 transplant" God is doing or has accomplished in your heart. (Psalm 37:4: "Delight yourself also in the Lord, and He shall give you the desires of your heart." See also Chapter 4, p. 60 of 2015 edition.) What desires of God growing in your heart does He want to bring to reality, or has He already achieved?

   ....

   ....

   ....

   ....

2. When has God done a "spiritual housecleaning" in your life? What difference did it make in your ability to walk in the light of Jesus?

   ....

   ....

   ....

   ....

3. Describe the difference between getting a glimpse of great things to do for God and getting a glimpse of what God wants to do through you. Why is this an important distinction?

   ....

   ....

   ....

   ....

4.   Do you have a vision from God that seems impossible for you to accomplish? "Write the vision" (see Habakkuk 2:2–3). What apparently impossible ministry, program, product, or service does God want to develop through you that is so excellent and unique people will say, "If you want that, you have to go to (your ministry or organization name)"?

_____

_____

_____

_____

5.   Is it true God gives big visions that are impossible for humans to accomplish? If so, why? Is God unreasonable? Give an example of a vision God gave you. Is it accomplished yet?

_____

_____

_____

_____

6.   During the Quest for Excellence journey, the author was transformed from a "Lord, I believe; help my unbelief" Christian into a "Wow! I'm amazed!" Christian (from p. 141; see Mark 9:24). Do you think the gift of faith enables obedience in the face of natural doubts? What doubts are you facing now?

_____

_____

_____

_____

LESSON FOUR

*"Enlarge the place of your tent, and let them stretch out
the curtains of your dwellings; do not spare; lengthen your cords,
and strengthen your stakes. For you shall expand to the
right and to the left, and your descendants will inherit the nations,
and make the desolate cities inhabited. Do not fear, for you will not be
ashamed; neither be disgraced, for you will not be put to shame...."*

—ISAIAH 54:2–4A

9. EXPECT CONFIRMATION – P. 187

God sometimes confirms His message through a persistent, deeper sense of "knowing," or He may speak through scripture reading or various circumstances of life. On occasion, He confirms His guidance through other people, and often through a combination of means. When you sense God is speaking, do not be afraid to ask Him for confirmation and correct understanding. Once you receive confirmation and correct understanding, move ahead in courage to obey what you have heard. When you have confidence about God's will for a particular situation, it becomes easier to persist in prayer, faith, and action toward its accomplishment. An often-repeated pattern for me is:

A. Confirmation through a passage of scripture that seems to come alive

B. Support from my wife, Kris, or other loved ones

C. The presence of a prayer burden for the project by our intercessory prayer group

D. Agreement by our administrative team and our Valley Christian Schools board

10. LET GOD SPEAK FOR HIMSELF – P. 97

Do not be surprised when you cannot convince others to support a God-sized project. After all, a rational person might tell you God's plans seem impossible. Trust that He knows how to communicate with people who are needed for the project in ways personally meaningful to them.

11. PAY THE PRICE – PP. 65-66

As God leads, be willing to sacrifice and give all toward the fulfillment of His purposes. When God wants to stretch your faith, the process is often uncomfortable, or even painful, requiring you to see and do things differently and seemingly unnaturally. It is not unusual for you, a rational person, to question your sanity; after all, Noah built an ark on dry ground when it had never rained in the history of the world. Or perhaps you resonate with Moses, who was tasked with leading millions of people across the Red Sea without a single boat; or with aged Abraham and barren Sarah trying to have as many children as there are stars in the sky and grains of sand on the seashore. Trust Him to take care of your needs and your reputation in pursuit of the vision. Take heed: The more vision God gives, the more you are responsible to accomplish what He has shown you. As Jesus said, ". . . to whom much is given, from him much will be required" (Luke 12:48).

12. WAIT UPON THE LORD – P. 148

Since only God can do His work, "wait on the Lord" to do it. You cannot force progress even if you try. Position yourself for God to act, then watch and wait expectantly for what God will do. Allow time for God to do His work in His way. Allow Him to teach you through trials and challenges. Wait, but do not give up on the vision. God often gives progressive disclosure to His vision. Oftentimes, the larger the vision, the longer the lead time between seeing the vision and doing the vision. The lead time allows for adequate prayer, personal spiritual growth, and planning.

We were led to purchase the land for Valley Christian Schools ten years before God opened the door for city approvals and for construction to begin. The Skyway campus vision seemed dead and buried. But about the time I began to question whether I had misunderstood God's vision, God powerfully resurrected the project. I have discovered that God often allows all to appear lost right before He shows up and does His miraculous work. I call them "Cliff hangers"! It is a great reminder that He is God and He uses these circumstances to grow our faith.

13. FORGET PLAN B – P. 149

Insist on going forward according to God's "A Team" plans. When obstacles or setbacks arise, pray and ask God to show you how He wants to deal with the situation. Believe that He does not want to settle for Plan B. Do not succumb to fear. God's vision is never lacking His provision. Be open to creative and unprecedented solutions. Remember, "Plans made in heaven are never ten feet too short!" (a Chapter 11 reference).

PERSONAL WRITTEN REFLECTIONS

1. What are some of the ways God gives confirmation of His leading to you and to others? Give one or more examples.

_____

_____

_____

_____

2. The decision to build the Skyway campus seemed unreasonable or irrational to many on the Valley Christian Schools board of directors, until God spoke to them through prayer (see pp. 95–98). Have you made a similar "illogical" decision based on God's leading, or are you facing such a decision now? Describe the experience. How do you receive the gift of faith in order to proceed?

_____

_____

_____

_____

3. When God asks you to step out in faith for an apparently impossible venture, what kind of fears are most difficult for you to navigate? Fear of failure? Fear of embarrassment or scorn? Based on Joshua 1:5–9 and Psalm 1:1–3, how can a godly person overcome fear?

_____

_____

_____

_____

DR. CLIFFORD E. DAUGHERTY

4.   What does it mean to wait on the Lord? Give an example from your experience or another person's experience.

5.   The greater the vision, it seems, the longer the lead time, allowing for more prayer time—do you agree or disagree? Discuss this idea, and give an example from Christian history or the Bible.

6.   When is it wise to have a Plan B, and when is it unwise? Give a real or hypothetical example for each case.

LESSON FIVE

"Do not forget to entertain strangers, for by so doing
some have unwittingly entertained angels."
—HEBREWS 13:2

14. CALL IN THE AIR FORCE – P. 70

The Bible refers to Satan as "the mighty prince of the power of the air" (Ephesians 2:2, NLT). The enemy always opposes God's work. Remember Paul's admonition: "For we are not fighting against people made of flesh and blood, but against the evil rulers and authorities of the unseen world, against those mighty powers of darkness who rule this world, and against wicked spirits in the heavenly realms" (Ephesians 6:12, NLT).

God appoints prayer intercessors to call in the "air cover" of His angelic hosts for His faithful warriors on the front lines. Watch for and honor the intercessors God assigns to pray for you and the vision you share. It is very helpful to pray weekly with an intercessory team as God leads. Keep your prayer team informed of your vision, your prayer requests, and how God is answering prayer, so they can pray strategically. Allow God to guide corporately as well as individually. "Pray at all times and on every occasion in the power of the Holy Spirit. Stay alert and be persistent in your prayers for all Christians everywhere. And pray for me, too" (Ephesians 6:18–19a, NLT).

The enemy is no match for God's angelic air force, and the Lord will defeat "the mighty prince of the power of the air" through prayer and the air cover of His angelic hosts. Every phase of God's work at Valley Christian Schools required a breakthrough in prayer to achieve success. When circumstances, human weaknesses, and dark forces seem to block God's purposes, partner with God-appointed prayer intercessors to call in the air force—God's angelic hosts!

"Praise Him, all His angels; praise Him, all His hosts!"
(Psalm 148:2).

"Restore us, O LORD God of hosts; cause
Your face to shine, and we shall be saved!"
(Psalm 80:19).

"The LORD of hosts is with us; the God of Jacob is our refuge"
(Psalm 46:11).

God assigns His angels to watch over us as children, and they are at His command to help us achieve His purposes throughout our lives as we pray and seek to serve Him. "See that you don't look down on one of these little ones, because I tell you that in heaven their angels continually view the face of My Father in heaven" (Matthew 18:10, HCSB).

(If you would like to study the subject of angels in more depth, see Billy Graham's book *Angels, Angels, Angels.*)

15. KEEP THE FAITH – P. 125

Do not allow obstacles to stop you or to damage your faith. Your faith will soar if instead you see obstacles as opportunities for God to demonstrate His miraculous power. Let Him reassure you about His desire and intention to accomplish His highest purposes in whatever way He chooses. Faith is a gift of the Holy Spirit, and God gives us the gift for each of His works. We cannot manufacture miracle-working faith. "The Spirit gives special faith . . ." (1 Corinthians 12:9, NLT).

DR. CLIFFORD E. DAUGHERTY

16. DUKE IT OUT – P. 169

Give yourself permission to wrestle with your doubts and to work through the "why" questions. Ask God to help you understand scriptural truths that apply to your situation. Ask God for the faith to make a wholehearted commitment to move forward in the face of unanswered questions like, "Where will we get the money?"

PERSONAL WRITTEN REFLECTIONS

1. Have you experienced an Ephesians 6:11–13 attack from the devil against your work for the Lord? Describe the attack, or an attack against another believer.

    ....

    ....

    ....

    ....

2. Did intercessory prayer as described in Ephesians 6:18–19 defeat the devil after the attack you described in Question 1, or have you had the privilege of praying for another Christian under attack? Describe such an experience and the result.

    ....

    ....

    ....

    ....

3. What role do you think God's heavenly host (angels) had in delivering you or your friend from the attack? See Daniel 9:21–23; 10:12–13, 19–20. According to Ephesians 6:19, what can we learn about how to pray for ministers of the gospel?

    ....

    ....

    ....

    ....

4. Based on 1 Corinthians 12:9 and 2 Corinthians 5:7, is the gift of faith given as the permanent possession of certain believers, or must faith be received as a gift repeatedly for each new challenge or endeavor? How do you experience it?

....

....

....

....

....

5. Is it beneficial or harmful to disclose your doubts about God's justice or goodness, or your pain about apparently unanswered prayers? Explain. How can the promise of James 1:5 help overcome doubts?

....

....

....

....

....

6. Would you agree or disagree that God's vision is never lacking His provision? Support your answer with scriptural insight.

....

....

....

....

LESSON SIX

"He who has begun a good work in you
will complete it until the day of Jesus Christ."
—PHILIPPIANS 1:6

17. TAP GREAT TALENT – P. 89

Ask God to help you do the homework needed to discover and engage the finest talent to help move the vision forward. Ask "the Lord of the harvest to send out laborers into His harvest" (Luke 10:2). The initial price tag is usually higher, but quality usually improves the bottom line before long.

18. NO SECRETS – P. 171

Always share the vision God gave you with those who will listen. On more than one occasion, I have shared God's vision with people of seemingly modest means who eventually gave tens of thousands—and even millions—of dollars in response to God's leading. Be faithful to share the vision, but understand that it is only God who can lead people to give their time, talent, and treasure from their hearts.

19. AIM FOR THE STARS – P. 61

Aim for excellence in everything you do. Ultimately, true excellence is the nature, character, and works of God. Anything we do truly reflecting excellence requires the work of God and is by definition "supernatural." Pursuing His excellence opens the door to experiencing His supernatural works in your everyday life—naturally.

20. JOURNAL THE JOURNEY – PP. 75-76

Periodically document the ways God has supernaturally worked through your life. Honor Him for His faithfulness, and allow these accounts to bring you and others into a new dimension of faith in and love for God. Later in life when you face doubts and difficulties, written testimonies of what God has accomplished through you will be a great encouragement. Recorded details of God's miraculous works will speak to you, your children, and their children, and teach others about His faithfulness.

PERSONAL WRITTEN REFLECTIONS

1. Are you comfortable finding people to support your work who are more talented than you are? Why or why not? What advice would you give to a leader who feels uncomfortable in such a situation?

_____

_____

_____

_____

2. Besides godly character, what are the most important four or five qualities you look for when building a successful team?

_____

_____

_____

_____

3. Are you comfortable sharing your God-given vision as well as the need for support from others in the form of time, talent, and treasure? How can someone uncomfortable with sharing the vision and its support needs gain the perspective to do so with confidence and enthusiasm?

_____

_____

_____

_____

4. Perhaps the phrase "living the supernatural life naturally" seems like an oxymoron. Is it? Why or why not?

....

....

....

....

5. Jesus said, "Therefore you shall be perfect, just as your Father in heaven is perfect" (Matthew 5:48). With this statement in view, when can believers become perfect and completely succeed in the Quest for Excellence? Take a look at 1 John 3:2, 2 Corinthians 5:21, and Romans 1:17.

....

....

....

....

6. How do you or will you journal your Quest for Excellence journey? For instance, the author writes journaling notes in a wide-margin Bible when God speaks a *rhema* word to him through scripture, then transfers the entries into an Excel spreadsheet with dates and reference verses.

....

....

....

....

....

My Personal Quest for Excellence

WRITTEN VISION STATEMENT

"Write the vision
And make it plain on tablets,
That he may run who reads it.
For the vision is yet for an appointed time;
But at the end it will speak, and it will not lie.
Though it tarries, wait for it;
Because it will surely come,
It will not tarry."

—HABAKKUK 2:2–3

Write a summary of the supernatural Quest for Excellence vision God is revealing to you. What does He plan to accomplish through your life during the next one year, three years, and perhaps ten years or more? Be prayerfully bold as you write! Give details as much as possible, including: What, When, Where, and How. Continue on additional pages as needed.

God willing, what vision will God accomplish through you during the next year?

God willing, what vision will God accomplish through you during the next three years?

God willing, what vision will God accomplish through you during the next ten years or more?

✳

MAY GOD BLESS

YOUR PERSONAL

QUEST FOR EXCELLENCE

AS YOU WALK

WITH JESUS!